DISASTERS

DEADLY STORMS

ANN WEIL

T0204275

SADDLEBACK
EDUCATIONAL PUBLISHING

DISASTERS

SADDLEBACK
EDUCATIONAL PUBLISHING
www.sdlback.com

ISBN-13: 978-1-61651-935-3
ISBN-10: 1-61651-935-5
eBook: 978-1-61247-631-5

Printed in the U.S.A.

21 20 19 18 17   5 6 7 8 9

Photo Credits: page 21, Jim McDonald/Corbis; page 47, Jim Zuckerman/
Corbis; page 51, AFP/Corbis; page 59, Corbis/Sygma; page 72, Hand-
out / Getty Images News / Getty Images; page 87, Kansas City Star /
McClatchy-Tribune / Getty Images

CONTENTS

DATAFILE

Timeline

September 12, 1988
Hurricane Gilbert strikes Jamaica with 125 mph gusts of wind.

December 27, 1998
A storm hits sailors in the Sydney to Hobart yacht race. Waves more than 80 feet high sweep sailors into the sea.

Where is Jamaica?

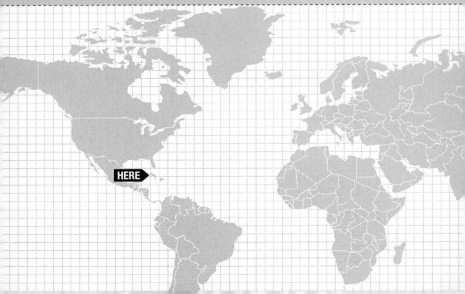

HERE

Key Terms

meteorologist—a specialist who reports, predicts, and studies the weather

storm surge—a mountain of water that occurs when a storm sucks up water from the ocean

tropical cyclone—a severe tropical storm with strong winds moving around a low-pressure center

CHAPTER 1 | Introduction

Bad weather happens all the time. Rain may spoil a picnic or ball game. Or it may be too cold and icy to play outside. Thunder and lightning can be frightening.

Most of the time, bad weather is just annoying. Sometimes, though, bad weather can be dangerous.

Storms can be killers. Many natural disasters are caused by bad weather. Strong winds can tear roofs off houses.

Trees can be ripped from the ground and tossed into the air. Cars and buses may be blown off the road. Heavy rains cause flooding. Bad floods can wash away entire villages. A storm at sea puts boats and sailors at risk.

Watching the Weather

Scientists who study the weather are called meteorologists. Many of them use computers and pictures from outer space to do their job.

They track storms and share their information with each other. Meteorologists can't control the weather, but they can often tell when and where a storm will strike.

Many people listen to weather reports on the radio. Television news programs include reports on the weather, too. Weather reports can be lifesavers. They warn people of bad storms heading their way. This gives people time to go somewhere safe to wait out the storm.

Tropical Storms

Tropical storms kill many thousands of people all over the world. These powerful storms begin in the warm ocean waters near the equator. The most severe tropical storms are called tropical cyclones.

Most tropical storms stay out at sea. Boats and ships may be at risk from these storms, but in general they cause very little damage. However, when a strong tropical storm strikes land, it can be a disaster.

Huge waves crash onto the shore. The storm sucks up water from the ocean. This mountain of water is called a storm surge. When the storm hits land, it brings this water with it. A storm surge can flood land near the coast. This is often the storm's biggest killer.

Meteorologists track tropical storms. They predict where the storm will go. Sometimes the storm changes course and strikes where no one expected.

But most of the time, people have some warning before a tropical storm hits land.

Some storms strike with little or no warning. Tornadoes are nature's most violent spinning storms. They have the fastest winds on Earth. Winds inside a tornado can whip around at 300 mph.

Tornadoes form inside thunderclouds. Then they dip down from the sky toward land. When a tornado touches down, it can cause tremendous damage.

A tornado is like a giant vacuum cleaner. It sucks up everything in its path. Houses, cars, people, and animals can all be pulled into the tornado.

The powerful winds rip things apart. Broken glass, wood, and metal whirl inside the tornado.

Most tornadoes do not last very long. Many disappear after only a few minutes. However, some can last for several hours.

Snow and Ice

Blizzards bury cars under hills of snow. Roofs can collapse under the weight of all that snow. People can be stuck in their homes with no way to leave. Icy roads make driving dangerous. Roads may be closed because it is not safe to drive.

Ice storms can bring down power lines. These wires can be deadly if someone accidentally touches them. Homes may be without electricity for days.

People can go without running water and heat. Their stoves and refrigerators don't work without electricity.

After the Storm

Large storms can do a lot of damage. It can take a long time to clean up after a storm.

First, rescue workers help survivors. Saving lives is the number one priority. People may be left homeless from the storm. They need food, water, and a new place to live. Then, power and phone lines need to be fixed. Roads must be cleared. Workers repair buildings and bridges.

Eventually, life returns to normal, until the next deadly storm hits.

Earth is not the only planet that has storms. Satellite photos show a storm like a hurricane on Jupiter. Scientists believe this storm has gone on for hundreds of years.

Hurricanes, Typhoons, and Cyclones

Hurricanes are tropical cyclones. Typhoons are also tropical cyclones. They are basically the same. The main difference between the two types is where they start. Hurricanes form in the Atlantic Ocean and the Caribbean. Typhoons begin in the Pacific Ocean. Storms beginning in the Indian Ocean are simply called cyclones.

DATAFILE

Timeline

November 13, 1970

A cyclone kills 500,000 people when it strikes the Ganges region.

April 29, 1991

A cyclone strikes Bangladesh and 250,000 die.

Where is Bangladesh?

Key Terms

cyclone shelter—a building raised high off the ground to avoid flood waters

Ganges region—the area near the Ganges River

tropical cyclone—a severe tropical storm with strong winds moving around a low-pressure center

CHAPTER 2 | Cyclones

Bad storms can strike any place, any time, but some places in the world have more deadly storms than others.

Cyclones

Cyclones form in the Indian Ocean. Storm surges from these severe tropical storms flood an area near the mouth of the Ganges River.

Bangladesh is a country in southern Asia. It is a very poor country. About 100 million people live in Bangladesh. Many of them struggle to feed themselves and their families.

The best place for them to grow food crops is near the Ganges River.

Storm surges and rains from tropical storms can cause serious flooding along river areas. Millions of people live along the banks of the Ganges River. Their lives are all at risk when a powerful cyclone strikes.

500,000 Die in 1970 Cyclone

One of the world's worst natural disasters happened in 1970. A powerful cyclone struck the Ganges region. The storm surge swept away homes and people.

Crops were destroyed. Millions of people were left homeless. There was no food to eat. Dead animals polluted the water. There was no clean water to drink. People who had survived the storm surge starved to death. Others got very sick from drinking the dirty water.

The Ganges region suffered many other cyclones. In 1985, water from a storm surge carried away homes and crops. Then, in 1991, there was a cyclone even more powerful than the one in 1970.

140,000 Die in 1991 Cyclone

The cyclone of 1991 killed almost 140,000 people. There were warnings before this cyclone hit. But many people did not have radios or televisions. They did not hear the warnings.

Other people did not believe the warnings. There had been other warnings and no cyclones had hit. They thought this was just another false alarm. But it wasn't.

This cyclone left about 10 million people homeless. Once again, there was no food or clean water to drink. People got very sick. Many died from starvation and disease.

Preparing for the Next Disaster

The people of Bangladesh must live with the threat of cyclones. They have built many large cyclone shelters to help more people survive these deadly storms. These shelters are special buildings raised high off the ground. People inside the shelters are above the flood waters.

Kolkata, India, 1737

About 300,000 died when a cyclone storm surge hit the Kolkata region of India.

Darwin, Australia, 1974

Cyclone Tracy struck Darwin, Australia, early Christmas morning, 1974. It almost destroyed the whole town. Only a few buildings were left standing.

Cyclone damage

DATAFILE

Timeline

September 21, 1938

A surprise hurricane strikes the northeastern
United States.

October 29, 1998

Hurricane Mitch strikes Central America.

Where is Central America?

HERE

Key Terms

eye—the center of the hurricane

hurricane—a tropical storm that begins in the Atlantic Ocean or Caribbean

mudslide—a huge amount of mud and rocks, which rolls rapidly down a hill

CHAPTER 3 | Hurricanes

Thunderclouds block the sun. Heavy rains pour from the sky, hour after hour. Violent winds bend trees to the breaking point and beyond. This is no ordinary thunderstorm. It's a hurricane.

Hurricanes are much more powerful than ordinary thunderstorms. They form in warm, tropical oceans.

Most hurricanes stay out at sea. Some hurricanes touch land. These can cause tremendous damage.

Huge waves can wash away houses—and people—too close to the shore. Strong winds tear trees out of the ground and blow cars off the road.

A mighty hurricane can flatten a whole town. Many people have been killed by hurricanes.

Inside a Hurricane

A hurricane has winds of at least 74 mph. These winds spin around the "eye," or center, of the storm.

The eye can be many miles wide. It is calm and quiet. The sky may be clear over the eye, too. People may think the storm has ended when the eye of the storm is passing over them.

This can be a deadly mistake. It is very dangerous to go out in the eye of the storm. The winds that whip around the eye are the most powerful of the storm.

A satellite view of a hurricane with the "eye" in the center.

Galveston, Texas, 1900

Galveston, Texas, is an island. It is connected to the rest of Texas by a bridge. Galveston has beautiful beaches. Many people enjoy vacations there.

On September 8, 1900, this pretty city was hit hard by a hurricane. Waves smashed the beaches. A 20-foot storm surge flooded the city.

The bridge was covered with water. People were trapped on the island as the water level continued to rise. Many people drowned.

The hurricane blew at about 115 mph. Water washed away the sand underneath the buildings. Houses collapsed.

About 6,000 people died in Galveston. Thousands more were killed by the same storm when it hit other islands and the mainland.

In Galveston, about 3,600 homes were lost. This left 10,000 people homeless. The city was destroyed.

A new Galveston was built. This time, there was a sea wall to help protect the city—and the people who lived there—from future storm surges.

The Great Hurricane of 1938

Some places have very few hurricanes. People who live there don't think these powerful storms will cause problems for them.

Unfortunately, some deadly storms strike where they are not expected. They catch people by surprise. This is what happened to people who lived in the northeastern part of the United States in 1938.

Mobile home park destroyed by a hurricane

This part of America hadn't seen a hurricane for many, many years. But a tropical storm was gathering speed in the Bahamas.

People expected the storm to blow out to sea. Instead it sped toward land.

The hurricane struck land at Long Island, New York, on September 21, 1938. People there were not prepared. There had been no warnings.

The storm blew across Long Island to Connecticut and Rhode Island. It was a strong hurricane with wind gusts of 150 mph.

A 20-foot storm surge swept the coast. 30-foot waves smashed against homes along the beaches. The storm also brought heavy rains to the whole Northeast. This added to the flooding caused by the storm surge.

More than 600 people died in this terrible storm. Thousands of homes were lost. Repairing the damage cost more than any other storm up till then.

Hurricane Mitch, 1998

Storms kill more people in poor countries. There is not enough money to build sturdy houses. The people may not have phones to call for help or radios and TVs to watch for storm warnings.

Rescue services in poor countries are not as well equipped as those found today in the United States. A bad hurricane in a poor country is more likely to cause a disaster.

Hurricane Mitch hit Central America on October 29, 1998. It brought 180 mph winds and heavy rains. The rain lasted for days.

More than 2 feet of water fell in a single 24-hour period. Hundreds of villages were flooded. Homes and other buildings were swept away by the water. Roads and bridges were washed out. There was no way for people to escape the floods.

The hurricane left about 10,000 dead and 2 million homeless in Honduras, Belize, Nicaragua, and Guatemala. Many of them drowned. Others died when mudslides buried their villages.

The worst mudslide happened near an old volcano. Part of the crater wall fell apart. An avalanche of mud, rocks, and trees rolled down the mountainside onto the villages below.

A survivor told of seeing parts of dead bodies poking up from the soft ground. About 1,500 people died this way. The actual number will never be known.

Naming Hurricanes

Americans started naming hurricanes in 1950 to keep track of the deadly storms. The first hurricane of the year is given a name beginning with the letter A. The second is given a name beginning with B, and so on.

A hurricane name is "retired" if the hurricane kills many people or causes a lot of damage. That name is not used again for another hurricane. Retiring hurricane names helps avoid confusing two hurricanes with the same name.

Some Retired Hurricane Names

Hurricane Camille was one of the strongest storms ever recorded. It struck land at Mississippi and Louisiana in 1969. More than 250 died.

Hurricane Gilbert struck the Caribbean and Mexico in 1988. It was one of the most powerful hurricanes ever recorded.

Hurricane Hugo stormed through the Caribbean in 1989. It killed dozens on several small Caribbean islands. It traveled on to the United States and struck South Carolina.

Hurricane Andrew was almost as powerful and destructive as Hurricane Camille. Winds of 150 mph and a 23-foot storm surge struck Eleuthera Island in the Bahamas. Damage on the islands was more than $250 million.

The hurricane continued on toward Florida. It smashed ashore near Homestead, Florida, on August 24, 1992. The killer storm continued through the Gulf of Mexico to Louisiana.

Hurricane Katrina was the most costly storm in American history.

DATAFILE

Timeline

March 18, 1925

The Tri-State Tornado tears through Missouri, Illinois, and Indiana.

April 11, 1965

Thirty-seven tornadoes hit Tornado Alley in only nine hours.

Where is Missouri?

HERE

Key Terms

funnel—the center part of the tornado

swarm—a group of tornadoes

terrorize—to fill with fear

tornado—a swirling mass of winds that sucks up everything in its path

CHAPTER 4 | Tornadoes

Tornadoes can be sudden and deadly. Most other storms form slowly. There is usually time to warn people. A tornado drops down from the clouds ready to destroy everything in its path.

Darkening Clouds

It is difficult to know when or where a tornado will strike. Sometimes people see dark clouds spinning in the sky before a tornado appears. The clouds may look green as well as gray and black.

A loud roar may come down from the sky, like the sound of a plane flying too close to the ground. Sometimes people see lightning in the clouds or inside the funnel of the tornado itself.

Tornadoes are smaller than hurricanes. However, they can pack more power. Size is not a good measure of a tornado's strength. A small tornado can be more powerful—and do more damage—than a large one.

Most tornadoes are quite weak. Their winds spin at about 40 mph. These tornadoes may knock over a tree or a traffic sign. People can be hurt when flying objects hit them.

Violent Winds

Violent tornadoes have winds as high as 300 mph. These monster tornadoes can tear houses apart. They can toss cars around as if they were toys. Heavy things, like refrigerators, can become deadly missiles.

Tornadoes disappear as suddenly as they appear. Sometimes they are gone after only a few seconds or minutes. A few tornadoes last as long as an hour or more. One of the longest tornadoes on record lasted three and a half hours. Tornadoes like that can travel as far as 100 miles.

Tornado Alley

Tornadoes can occur in many parts of the world. The United States has more tornadoes than other countries. There are about 1,000 tornadoes in the United States every year.

No place is safe from tornadoes. Big cities, like Ft. Worth, Texas, have been hit by a tornado. Even the suburbs of Washington, DC, have the occasional tornado. In September 2001, two sisters were killed by a tornado. They were inside a car when the tornado whipped through the University of Maryland, near Washington, DC. The tornado picked up the car and threw it around.

Some states in America have more tornadoes than others. Most tornadoes happen in Tornado Alley.

Tornado Alley is in the central part of the United States. It is a large area that includes many states. There are cities and small towns in Tornado Alley. There are a lot of farms, too.

Tornadoes usually happen in the spring and summer. This is when the weather is very warm and wet. There are tornadoes almost every week during this time. Tornado Alley has about 700 tornadoes a year. Sometimes many tornadoes appear at once. These groups of tornadoes are called "swarms."

Staying Safe

The safest place to be when a tornado hits is underground. Many houses in Tornado Alley have strong basements. When people see a tornado coming, they can run into one of these shelters.

A bad place to hide is inside a car. A car is not a safe place to be when a tornado is coming.

Tri-State Tornado, March 1925

The worst tornado disaster happened in March 1925. A tornado traveled

Two hundred nineteen miles through three Midwestern states. It became known as the Tri-State Tornado.

The Tri-State Tornado was the deadliest tornado in America's history. Six hundred ninety-five people were killed. Two thousand were injured. Houses and farms were destroyed.

This tornado formed in the skies over Missouri. It touched down and killed 11 in that state.

Then it crossed the border into Illinois. It went through the town of Gorham. The tornado killed or injured about half the people who lived or worked there.

The tornado moved on through Illinois and into Indiana. It struck several mining towns along the way. Schools were torn apart. Many children were killed.

The tornado went through Princeton, Indiana. Then it disappeared.

The tornado had traveled at about 62 mph. That's approximately the speed of a car on the highway. No tornado before had ever gone so fast and so far, or killed so many.

"Super Outbreak" April 1974

Sometimes several tornadoes start at once. Over a period of two days in April 1974, 148 killer tornadoes terrorized parts of the United States and Canada.

For about six hours, a new tornado appeared every few minutes. Tornadoes were reported in 13 states and two Canadian provinces.

A mile-wide tornado ripped through the large town of Xenia, Ohio. The tornado blew apart schools and churches. Stores and shops were smashed to bits.

A freight train was traveling through Xenia when the tornado hit. The tornado knocked the train over, as if it were a toy.

The tornado destroyed half of the town. Thirty-three people were killed in Xenia. 10,000 people were left homeless.

Trying to help the survivors was difficult because of the tornado damage. The fallen train blocked the way fire trucks and ambulances needed to go.

There were also killer tornadoes in Kentucky, Indiana, Tennessee, and Alabama. Altogether, this swarm of tornadoes killed more than 300 people.

Waco, Texas, 1953

A huge tornado hit the city of Waco, Texas, on May 11, 1953. It killed 114 people. About 600 more were injured.

The tornado blew buildings apart. Bricks rained down on the street below. Cars and people were crushed. Some survivors were rescued after being buried alive for more than 12 hours.

Tornado Alley, 1965

A swarm of 37 tornadoes terrorized the people of Tornado Alley for nine hours. Two hundred seventy-one were killed.

Wichita Falls, Texas, 1979

A one-mile-wide tornado ripped through the town of Wichita Falls on April 10, 1979. It left 42 people dead and 20,000 homeless. This tornado was part of a swarm that touched down in Texas and Oklahoma that day.

Kansas and Oklahoma, 1991

A swarm of tornadoes struck Kansas and Oklahoma in April 1991. It destroyed many houses and hundreds of mobile homes. More than 30 people were killed. Hundreds were injured.

Jarrell, Texas, 1997

A tornado cut through the town of Jarrell on May 27, 1997. The tornado killed at least 32 people.

Arkansas and Tennessee, 1999

Swarms of tornadoes hit Arkansas and Tennessee in January 1999. 169 separate tornadoes were reported.

Oklahoma City, 1999

A swarm of over 50 violent tornadoes ripped through four states. The area around Oklahoma City was hit hard with more than $1 billion damage.

Eastern States, 2002

A swarm of very powerful tornadoes ripped through the eastern United States in November 2002. Tennessee and Alabama were hard hit. Ohio, Pennsylvania, and Mississippi were also affected by the storms. Dozens of people were reported killed or missing. Some of them were rescue workers.

Kansas to Georgia, 2003

Three hundred eighty-four tornadoes raged through 19 states during the week of May 4, 2003. This total set a new record.

Damage from the 1999 Oklahoma tornado

DATAFILE

Timeline

October 27, 1991

The "Halloween Storm" begins as a hurricane.

March 12–13, 1993

The "Storm of the Century" strikes the United States, killing more than 300 people.

Where is New England?

Key Terms

New England—the name given to the most northeastern states: Connecticut, Rhode Island, Massachusetts, New Hampshire, Vermont, and Maine

Nor'easter—a storm in New England that brings heavy rains

CHAPTER 5 | The Perfect Storm

New England is used to storms called "Nor'easters." Winds blow in from the northeast. Nor'easters bring heavy rains and rough seas. Nor'easters are very bad news for boats at sea.

The Halloween Storm

The "Halloween Storm" of 1991 was much worse than any Nor'easter. It was the "perfect storm."

It was "perfect" because so many different things happened together. The perfect storm started with Hurricane Grace. It formed on October 27, 1991.

Scientists watched the hurricane on their computer screens. It moved up the east coast from Bermuda. The scientists were amazed at what they saw.

Several storm systems combined with the hurricane. Cold air was coming down from Canada. Huge waves smashed the East Coast, from North Carolina up to Nova Scotia, Canada. After a few days, the hurricane became weaker. But the Halloween Storm grew stronger.

The Halloween Storm killed six fishermen on the boat, *Andrea Gail*. Their story was turned into a book and a movie, both called *The Perfect Storm*.

The Halloween Storm killed others, too. Two men drowned off Staten Island, New York, when their boat turned over in the storm.

Most people know how dangerous it is to be near the shore during a big storm. Some people ignore the danger and pay with their lives.

A man in Rhode Island was fishing during the storm. Big waves washed him off the rocks and he drowned. The storm killed a man in New York who was fishing from a bridge. He was either blown off the bridge by the strong winds or swept away by the water.

The storm caused a lot of damage. Homes and businesses in New England were ruined. Land near the coast was flooded. Roads and airports were forced to close.

Finally, the Halloween Storm got weaker. As the perfect storm died, a new hurricane formed at its center.

Since 1950, almost all hurricanes have been named. This new hurricane was an exception. It never received a name.

There was a good reason for this. People were still talking about the Halloween Storm. Naming the new hurricane might confuse them.

The no-name hurricane blew out to sea. The Halloween Storm was over.

This scene from the movie *The Perfect Storm* shows the boat in the crashing waves created by the storm.

"Storm of the Century"

In March 1993, a huge storm closed down the East Coast of the United States for several days. It was called "The Storm of the Century."

Tornadoes, high winds, and very heavy snows stretched from Florida up to the Northeast. Forty-four people were killed by a swarm of tornadoes in Florida. Wind speeds reached 100 mph.

The storm blew down trees and power lines. Millions of people had no electricity in their homes. Roads and airports were closed. Snow fell on parts of the southern United States that almost never get snow.

Farther north, the snow fell at a rate of about two to three inches an hour. Some places got more than three feet of snow.

The storm claimed 270 lives on land. Forty-eight people were missing at sea. It cost billions of dollars to repair the damage caused by the Storm of the Century.

DATAFILE

Timeline

September 9, 1965

Hurricane Betsy brings torrential rain and 110 miles per hour winds to Louisiana. Levees around New Orleans fail, flooding the city for over ten days.

August 29, 2005

Hurricane Katrina hits the Gulf Coast with winds of over 150 miles per hour.

Where is the Gulf Coast?

Key Terms

landfall—arrival on land

levee—a wall of earth or stone built to prevent flooding from a river

mandatory evacuation—leaders emphasize leaving an unsafe location and limit entry into that location

CHAPTER 6 | Hurricane Katrina

On the morning of August 29, 2005, one of the worst hurricanes to hit the US in the last 100 years struck the Gulf Coast. It was named Hurricane Katrina. This storm devastated parts of Louisiana, Mississippi, Alabama, and Florida. Katrina would go down in history as the storm that drowned a city.

Katrina was initially a simple tropical depression. It was located just south of the Bahamas. Tropical depressions have winds of 38 miles per hour or less. But scientists with the National Hurricane Center continued to keep an eye on this one. The center's computers showed the tropical depression was strengthening.

Two days later, the tropical depression intensified into a tropical storm. Its wind speed was close to 70 miles per hour. As the storm spun its way toward Florida, it gathered more energy from the warm Gulf water. Scientists quickly reclassified the storm as a hurricane. The National Weather Service named it Katrina.

On August 25, 2005, Katrina touched the eastern shore of Florida. More than five inches of rain fell along its path, causing widespread flooding. Some areas received as much as 15 inches of rain. Winds topped 80 miles per hour. Four people died and more than one million were without power.

Max Mayfield was the director of the National Hurricane Center. He had worked at the center for more than 30 years. Mayfield was an expert in predicting hurricanes. As he watched computer models of Katrina, he got very worried. The hurricane was changing course. And it was gaining power.

Mayfield decided to do something he had never done before. He placed an emergency call to the governors of Mississippi and Louisiana. Mayfield told them that Hurricane Katrina was going to cause devastating damage to their states. They should work up an evacuation plan.

As Katrina continued to pound Florida, scientists boarded specially equipped planes. The plan was to fly directly into the hurricane. This was no foolish adventure. These scientists wanted to measure Katrina's wind speeds, humidity, and the local water temperatures among other data.

On Sunday, August 28, Katrina headed toward Louisiana and Mississippi. It quickly strengthened into a Category 5 hurricane, the highest rating possible. Katrina now had winds over 175 miles per hour.

Ray Nagin was the mayor of New Orleans. On Sunday morning, August 28, he ordered a mandatory evacuation of his city. People complained that they wanted to stay in their homes. But Mayor Nagin insisted they evacuate. Their lives were in danger.

Thousands of people drove, took buses, and walked out of the city. As many as one million residents of New Orleans and its suburbs evacuated. But more than 100,000 remained. Some did not own cars. Others could not afford bus fare. They were trapped as Hurricane Katrina barreled toward them.

The Superdome was declared a shelter of last resort for those who were still in the city. The Superdome is the major sports stadium in New Orleans. Food and water were taken there to prepare. But more than 10,000 people arrived the night before the storm hit. There was only enough water for one day.

On Monday, August 29, at 5:10 a.m., Katrina made landfall in Mississippi and Louisiana. Winds roared in at over 150 miles per hour. Windows blew out of high-rise buildings. Shards of glass were flung through the streets by hurricane-force winds.

In the Superdome, winds over 100 miles per hour were tearing at the roof. Parts of it were ripped off and rain fell in. There was no air conditioning. Toilets were overflowing.

Heavy rains flooded streets and homes. Electricity went out. The storm knocked out telephone and cellular service as well as Internet access. Despite the drenching rains, fires broke out across the city. Many were lighting candles because they had no electricity.

In Alabama, hurricane-force winds created storm surges over 13 feet high. Shrimp boats were dragged onto shore and crushed. Marinas were destroyed as well as beachfront homes and hotels. Major highways were completely submerged. More than 500,000 residents lost power.

In Mississippi, a 27-foot storm surge reached up to 12 miles inland. Nearly 1.5 million acres of forest were destroyed. Governor Haley Barbour said that Hurricane Katrina hit Mississippi "like a ton of bricks." All the counties in Mississippi were declared disaster areas.

Later, on the morning of landfall, Katrina continued to pound the city with rains and hurricane winds. The levees in New Orleans were breached around 11:00 a.m. Levees are barriers of dirt and concrete that protect cities from flooding.

Soon, 80 percent of the city was flooded. Muddy, contaminated water poured through the streets. Trees and power lines toppled over roads. Water rose to the tops of roofs.

Public health emergencies were declared in Louisiana, Mississippi, Alabama, and Florida. Flood waters were carrying toxic chemicals and bacteria through the streets. Katrina had destroyed many sanitation facilities. The water was now contaminated with raw sewage and human waste.

Poor communities like St. Bernard Parish and the Ninth Ward were especially devastated. Almost every single house was submerged in St. Bernard Parish. In the Ninth Ward, flood waters ripped apart homes and buried cars in mud and contaminated water.

Survival

Residents in New Orleans dragged themselves through polluted water looking for higher ground. But roads were torn away or flooded. Shelters were destroyed. People had no food or water. The sick and the elderly in local hospitals were being flown to safer areas in helicopters and military planes.

Panicked survivors climbed to the roofs of buildings. But now they were exposed to the elements. Temperatures and humidity levels were rising. It was close to 100 degrees. Children and the elderly were at risk for heat stroke.

Crowds of frantic residents waited for emergency crews that were delayed by flooded roads. When police arrived, there was mass confusion. Riots broke out as residents lined up for food and water. There were not enough supplies.

Flooded roadways can be seen in New Orleans, Louisiana, after Katrina made landfall.

Thousands more pushed through dirty, snake-infested water to get to a building where they thought they could get help: the Superdome.

With the Superdome overwhelmed, police were directing survivors to the Convention Center. Thousands went there seeking assistance, but there was none. The Superdome quickly filled with the injured and hungry.

Finally, Louisiana Governor Kathleen Blanco sent in the National Guard. Troops drove into the city with medical supplies, food, clothing, and water. They also constructed tents for temporary shelters. But despite their efforts, more than 600 people died that first day in Louisiana.

Economic Impact

Katrina's winds battered the Gulf Coast and damaged offshore oil rigs. The Gulf Coast oil industry produces more than 30 percent of our oil and 20 percent of our natural gas. After Katrina hit, oil prices started to rise sharply. Overall economic damage from Katrina topped $100 billion.

The Aftermath

Years after Katrina, officials still don't have exact figures of the number of dead and missing. In Louisiana, more than 1,500 were declared dead or missing. In Mississippi, nearly 250 died. Hundreds are still missing and may never be accounted for.

Before Katrina wiped out large parts of New Orleans, the city had a population of 485,000. A recent survey put the number of residents today at just over 340,000. New Orleans's population has shrunk by approximately 30 percent in just a few years.

Many scientists believe global warming is making natural disasters worse. With sea levels rising, more cities on the coasts are vulnerable to hurricanes and flooding. Warmer ocean waters are a breeding ground for hurricanes. With better forecasting, scientists hope we can plan our responses better. We need to prepare for the natural disasters that are in our future.

DATAFILE

Timeline

1946

Joplin, Missouri, acquires national awareness with its mention in the iconic road song "Route 66."

May 22, 2011

Warning sirens signal the approaching tornado that eventually becomes a powerful and deadly EF-5 storm.

Where is Joplin, Missouri?

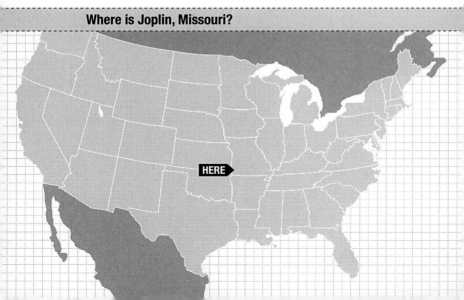

HERE

Key Terms

generator—a machine that converts one form of energy into another

intensify—to make stronger, increase

meteorologist—a specialist who reports, predicts, and studies the weather

CHAPTER 7 | Joplin's EF-5 Tornado

Joplin, Missouri, is a small city of 50,000 located in the southwestern part of Missouri. It is near the edge of the Ozark Mountain range. Missouri is part of the Four-State region, which includes Missouri, Oklahoma, Kansas, and Arkansas. Every year, many tornadoes touch down in the Four-State region.

In the spring of 2011, the Midwest and South were experiencing high temperatures and hardly any rain. These conditions set up a pattern of severe weather. Thunderstorms and a series of tornadoes cropped up in the area from central Texas, through the Four-State region and the South, all the way to the East Coast.

The Big One Hits

On Sunday, May 22, meteorologists warned of a severe weather system heading toward Joplin. Skies darkened in the city. There were rumbles of thunder. Lightning bolts lit up the sky.

Tornado warning sirens sounded. But many Joplin residents didn't pay attention. Sirens are used often in the Four-State area. People have become used to them. Sirens went off earlier for a different storm. People thought the danger was over.

Later, around 5:34 p.m., a massive tornado touched down to the west of town. Joplin residents were just sitting down for dinner. The sirens sounded again at 5:38 p.m. Some residents could not hear the sirens because of the storm's loud winds.

People who heard the first warning sirens had only 20 minutes' notice before the tornado hit. Houses started to shake. Windows shattered and lights flickered on and off.

Meteorologists reported that Joplin was experiencing a "supercell" storm. Supercells are some of the most dangerous storms. They form when cold, dry weather systems and warm, humid systems crash together. Supercells can inflict serious damage when they hit.

Residents looked out of their windows to see how bad the storm was. But they could not see it. The storm had intensified into a tornado. It was wrapped in a thick blanket of rain. From the windows, the tornado just looked like a massive dark cloud. But Joplin was in the path of the deadliest tornado in its history.

There was no time for an evacuation. Joplin residents ran to their basements or bathrooms. Roaring winds rocked houses and tore off roofs. With no power or telephone service, residents did not know how bad the tornado was. In the center of Joplin, the tornado was passing through at 20 miles per hour. Streets emptied as residents ran for cover.

The Joplin tornado started to strengthen. It was three-quarters of a mile across and left a trail of devastation 13 miles long. Cars and trucks were tossed in the air. Some vehicles flew several blocks before crashing into buildings. Winds stripped the bark right off trees then snapped them like twigs. In minutes, hundreds of homes were gone.

The destruction kept getting worse. Tornado winds were now measuring over 200 miles per hour. Later, meteorologists classified the Joplin tornado as an EF-5. This was the highest rating given to tornadoes.

As every minute passed, the Joplin tornado swept across more of the city. Homes flew off foundations. Street signs and pieces of cars and trucks whipped through the air. Lashing gusts of wind made it hard to see.

At 6:00 p.m., the tornado had passed. Power had been lost. The only lights in Joplin were from fire trucks and police cars. Phones were not working. There was no Internet service. The governor of Missouri called in the National Guard.

Many rescue vehicles had been damaged. This severely slowed down Joplin's rescue operations. Police were ordering residents to stay off the streets. There were downed power lines that could electrocute people. Police also had the sad task of locating bodies in homes and businesses.

Police and firefighters were pulling survivors from crushed homes. Sparks flew from downed power lines. Gas lines ruptured, and flames shot into the dark sky. Tractor-trailers had overturned on the highways. Access was blocked for hospital and emergency vehicles.

A Hospital Tragedy

The Joplin tornado devastated St. John's Hospital. It was the principal hospital in Joplin. Every window blew out. Patients and staff were cut by flying glass. Some patients were knocked out of their beds. More than 180 patients and staff took cover inside stairwells as the building shook. Chunks of concrete and glass fell from the hospital's top floors. Walls were collapsing.

Doctors and nurses led healthier patients down to the lobby. They set up beds for the injured. Those left on upper floors were the sickest patients. They were not healthy enough to walk to safety. Lights went off and most elevators stopped working. Heroically, nurses and doctors started leading every one of the sickest patients to the lobby

But there were still critically sick patients to deal with. Many could not breathe on their own. They needed breathing machines called ventilators. As tornado winds tore through the floors, the hospital's generator was ripped out of the building. Every piece of electrical equipment stopped working.

Hospital staff flipped the switch on the emergency generator. But it didn't work. They tried another backup generator. That didn't work either.

The ventilator machines were no longer operating. Nurses tried physically pumping the ventilators themselves. But it wasn't enough. Five patients in critical condition died because their ventilators stopped working.

Minutes Felt Like Hours

Most tornadoes last an average of ten minutes. The 2011 Joplin tornado lasted just over 30 minutes. The destruction was unbelievable. Residents staggered from their homes to find neighborhoods completely flattened. From inside houses, people screamed for help. Others used crowbars to pry their front doors open.

Many familiar Joplin landmarks were gone. Favorite stores were nothing but piles of cement and glass. Survivors could not get supplies like food and water. More than 75 percent of Joplin was demolished in less than 30 minutes.

The Aftermath

Throughout the night, rescue crews picked through the debris with their bare hands. They were careful not to use heavy equipment right away. Pushing debris with large bulldozers and trucks can cause heavily damaged buildings to collapse. Any survivors inside the building could die.

Rains poured down on police and firefighters as they worked. Dark clouds framed mounds of crushed cars piled on top of one another. Joplin had been in the direct eye of the tornado. The tornado